BEWARE
SURPRISES
AHEAD

My name is

_____

I am _____ years old

    and in grade _____

My best friend is

_____

I live in Canada: yes   no

    I have lived here for_____

Sleeping Bear Press™

315 E. Eisenhower Parkway, Suite 200
Ann Arbor MI 48108
www.sleepingbearpress.com

Sleeping Bear Press is an imprint of Gale, a part of Cengage Learning.

10 9 8 7 6 5 4 3 2 1

ISBN 978-1-58536-812-9

Printed by China Translation & Printing Services Limited,
Guangdong Province,China. 1st printing. 02/2012

Diary of a Canadian Kid

Artwork by Cyd Moore

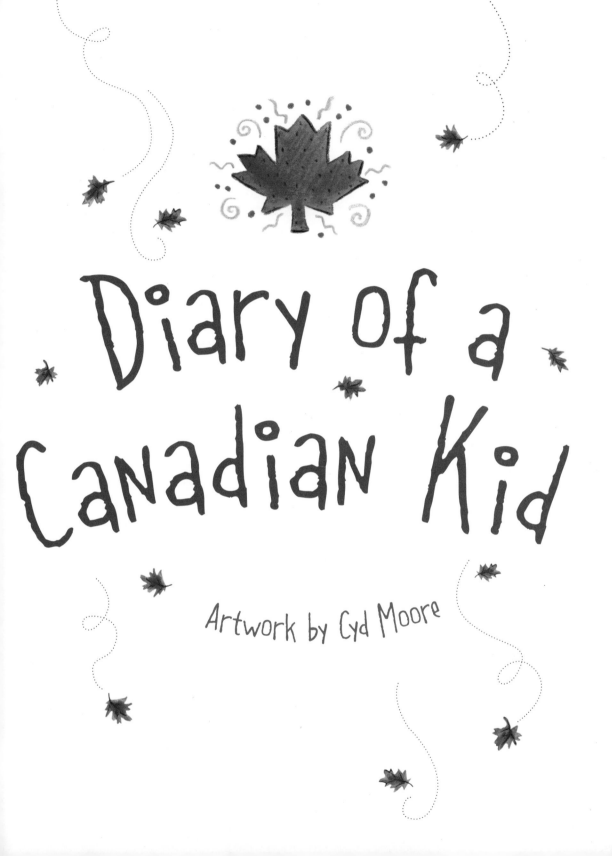

Russia

North Pole ↑

Beaufort Sea

Banks

Alaska USA

Victoria Island

Yukon Territory

whitehorse

Echo Bay

Northwest Territories

N

yellowknife

British Columbia

Alberta

Saskatchewan

Prince George

Edmonton

Calgary

M

Pacific Ocean

Victoria →

Vancouver

Saskatoon

Regina

Winni

Where Do YOU Live in Canada?

4

USA

smere Island

Greenland

Greenland
Sea

Baffin
Bay

Iceland

Baffin Island

Davis
Strait

ut

Iqaluit

Labrador Sea

er

Ivujivik

Newfoundland
and Labrador

a

Hudson
Bay

Quebec

St.
John's

Ontario*

Thunder Bay

Quebec

Prince Edward
Island

Montreal

Nova Scotia
Halifax

Ottawa

New Brunswick

Great
Lakes

Toronto

Atlantic Ocean

5

WRITE!

Today's date: _____

_____

_____

_____

_____

_____

_____

_____

_____

_____

_____

_____

_____

_____

_____

_____

_____

_____

DRAW!

Today's date: _____

The great country of Canada!

Are you a Canadian kid?
How many national facts do
you already know? See if you
can fill in the right answers!
(The correct answers are at the bottom
on the next page.)

National tree:

_____

National animal:

_____

National colours:

_____

National anthem:

_____

National motto:

_____

Nation's first prime minister

_____

National capital:

_____

Official winter sport:

_____

Official summer sport:

_____

Tree: Maple Tree • *Animal:* Beaver • *Colours:* Red & White • *Anthem:* O Canada • *Motto:* From Sea to Sea (A mari usqu ad mare) • *Prime Minister:* Sir John A. Macdonald • *Capital:* Ottawa, Ontario • *Winter Sport:* Ice Hockey • *Summer Sport:* Lacrosse

WRITE!

Today's date: _____

_____

_____

_____

_____

_____

_____

_____

_____

_____

_____

_____

_____

_____

_____

_____

DRAW!

Today's date: _____

Today we went to

_____

_____

_____

_____

My favourite thing about today was

_____

_____

_____

_____

_____

_____

_____

My least favourite thing about today was

_____

_____

_____

_____

_____

_____

_____

_____

_____

Would I visit here again? Why or why not?

_____

_____

_____

_____

_____

WRITE!

Today's date: _____

_____

_____

_____

_____

_____

_____

_____

_____

_____

_____

_____

_____

_____

_____

_____

DRAW!

Today's date: _____

From our National Maple Tree comes
Maple Syrup!

Canada is well known for its maple syrup made from the sap that comes from our national tree—the maple tree. Sap is a watery solution of sugars that is formed within the tree. In the early spring this solution is collected by a system called tapping. Tapping is done by drilling a hole and inserting a metal or plastic spout into the tree for the sap to drip out into a bucket. After the sap is collected, it is boiled to create the perfect colour, texture, and flavour of maple syrup.

Maple Syrup Festivals are held every year across Canada. At these festivals you can help make maple syrup.

What do you eat with maple syrup?

Pancake Recipe

- 1 cup (250 ml) all-purpose flour
- 1 tablespoon (15 ml) white sugar
- 1 teaspoon (5 ml) baking powder
- ½ teaspoon (2 ml) baking soda
- ¼ teaspoon (1 ml) salt
- 1 cup (250 ml) milk
- 1 egg
- 2 tablespoons (30 ml) vegetable oil

Directions:

1. Preheat a lightly oiled griddle over medium-high heat.

2. Combine flour, sugar, baking powder, baking soda, and salt. Make a well in the centre.

3. In a separate bowl, beat together egg, milk, and oil. Pour milk mixture into flour mixture. Beat until smooth. You can add blueberries or chocolate chips here if you like!

4. Pour or scoop the batter onto the hot griddle, using approximately ¼ cup (50 ml) for each pancake. Brown on both sides and serve hot.

5. Pour on maple syrup and enjoy!

23

WRITE!

Today's date: _____

_____

_____

_____

_____

_____

_____

_____

_____

_____

_____

_____

_____

_____

_____

_____

DRAW!

-long
-grey

-in a box? -Henry/dad said

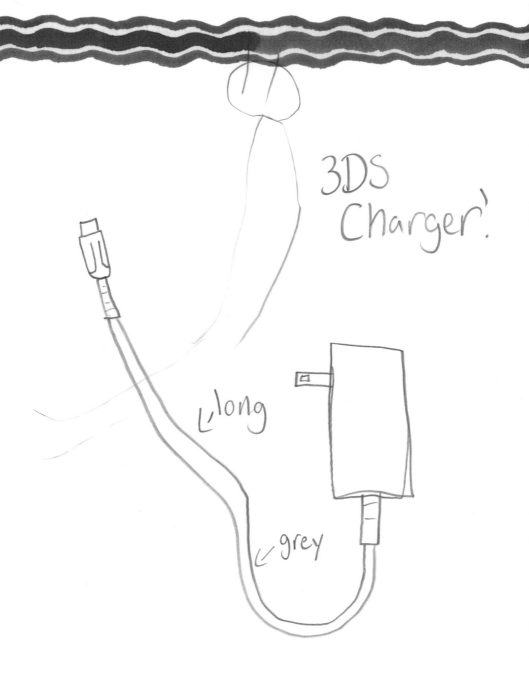

3DS
Charger!

long

grey

The proud symbol of Canada:
The Canadian flag!

Did you know that it wasn't until February 15, 1965 that Canada officially proclaimed a National Flag of Canada? Today this date is celebrated as National Flag of Canada Day. The Canadian flag contains the two official colours of Canada—red and white. Centred on a white background is an eleven point red maple leaf with a red border on the right and left edge of the flag.

The Canadian flag can often be found flying high on top of tall buildings, being waved joyfully on Canada Day, July 1, even blowing in the wind from the rafters of your own home or your neighbour's house.

On July 1, 1980 "O Canada" was declared our official national anthem. Canada has two official languages: English and French. The music for "O Canada" was composed by Calixa Lavallee. English lyrics were written by Robert Stanley Weir and French lyrics were written by Adolphe-Basile Routhier.

Official English

O Canada!
Our home and native land!
True patriot love in all thy sons command.
With glowing hearts we see thee rise,
The True North strong and free!
From far and wide,
O Canada, we stand on guard for thee.
God keep our land glorious and free!
O Canada, we stand on guard for thee.
O Canada, we stand on guard for thee.

Official French

Ô Canada!
Terre de nos aïeux,
Ton front est ceint de fleurons glorieux!
Car ton bras sait porter l'épée,
Il sait porter la croix!
Ton histoire est une épopée
Des plus brillants exploits.
Et ta valeur, de foi trempée,
Protégera nos foyers et nos droits.
Protégera nos foyers et nos droits.

WRITE!

Today's date: _____

What can I do to make
Canada a better place?

_____

_____

_____

_____

_____

_____

_____

_____

_____

_____

_____

_____

DRAW!

Today's date: _____

Let's play some games!

Going on a trip?

Here are some fun games to play on your next road trip.

Scavenger Hunt

Before you start out on your trip, make a list of items and places you might see along the way (11 blue cars, 2 bridges, 5 motels, 3 towns that have 10 letters in their names, etc.). Check them off as you find them.

What is the funniest town name you've ever heard?

_____

_____

_____

_____

_____

If you were going to name a town, what would it be?

_____

_____

Licence Plate Game

Make a list of all the provinces and territories. See how many different state licence plates you can find, and check them off your list.(Variation: Keep a list of all the vanity plates you find.)

Make up your own funny licence plates.

Auto Tag

Each person chooses a symbol or something you are likely to encounter regularly on the road, such as a gas station logo, a restaurant sign, a farm animal, a motorcycle. When a player sees her item, she calls it out and gently tags the next player, who then proceeds to search for his symbol, and so on.

WRITE!

Today's date: _____

_____

_____

_____

_____

_____

_____

_____

_____

_____

_____

_____

_____

_____

DRAW!

Today's date: _____

Today we went to

_____

_____

_____

_____

_____

My favourite thing about today was

_____

_____

_____

_____

_____

_____

_____

_____

My least favourite thing about today was

_____

_____

_____

_____

_____

_____

_____

_____

Would I visit here again? Why or why not?

_____

_____

_____

_____

_____

_____

WRITE!

Today's date: _____

_____

_____

_____

_____

_____

_____

_____

_____

_____

_____

_____

_____

_____

DRAW!

Today's date: _____

Let's play a sport!

In 1994 ice hockey was declared the national winter sport and lacrosse the national summer sport of Canada.

What sports do you like?

☐ Hockey   ☐ Tennis   ☐ Running

☐ Lacrosse   ☐ Curling   ☐ Hiking

☐ Baseball   ☐ Figure Skating   ☐ Biking

☐ Soccer   ☐ Gymnastics   ☐ Other_____

The National Hockey League (NHL) was formed in November 1917 and consisted of five Canadian teams—the Ottawa Senators, the Quebec Bulldogs, the Montreal Canadiens, the Montreal Wanderers, and the Toronto Arenas. Today 30 NHL teams compete for the Stanley Cup.

Lacrosse is one of the oldest sports in Canada. It is believed our First Nations played the game more than 500 years ago. Played with a stick with a netted pouch at the end and a rubber ball, the object of the game is to score points by shooting the ball into the other team's goal.

How many hockey or lacrosse team names do you know?

_____

_____

_____

_____

What is your favourite team?

_____

Design your own team's jersey. Maybe it's bold and powerful or wacky and playful. You be the designer!

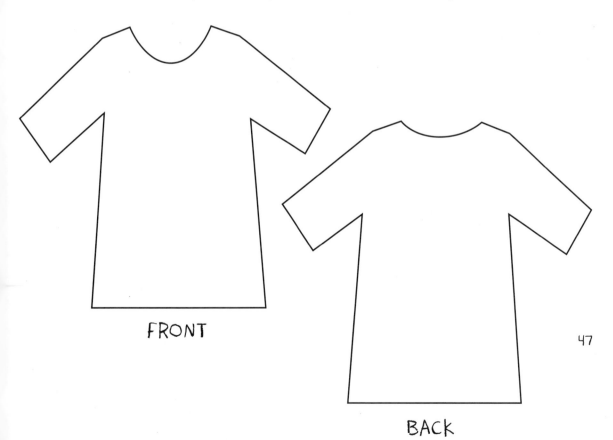

FRONT

BACK

WRITE!

Today's date: _____

Who is my favourite Canadian?

_____

_____

_____

_____

_____

_____

_____

_____

_____

_____

_____

_____

_____

_____

_____

DRAW!

Today's date: _____

When it rains,
my favourite things to do:

_____

_____

_____

_____

_____

_____

_____

_____

_____

_____

_____

Favourite movie

_____
_____
_____

Favourite TV show

_____
_____
_____

Favourite video game

_____
_____
_____

Favourite book

_____
_____
_____

Favourite art projects

_____

_____

WRITE!

Today's date: _____

_____

_____

_____

_____

_____

_____

_____

_____

_____

_____

_____

_____

_____

_____

_____

_____

_____

DRAW!

Today's date: _____

Today we went to

_____

_____

_____

_____

My favourite thing about today was

_____

_____

_____

_____

_____

_____

_____

_____

My least favourite thing about today was

Would I visit here again? Why or why not?

WRITE!

Today's date: _____

_____

_____

_____

_____

_____

_____

_____

_____

_____

_____

_____

_____

_____

_____

_____

DRAW!

Today's date: _____

Today we went to

_____

_____

_____

_____

_____

My favourite thing about today was

_____

_____

_____

_____

_____

_____

_____

_____

_____

My least favourite thing about today was

Would I visit here again? Why or why not?

WRITE!

Today's date: _____

_____

_____

_____

_____

_____

_____

_____

_____

_____

_____

_____

_____

_____

_____

_____

_____

DRAW!

Today's date: _____

Let's play MORE GAMES!

Billboard Poetry

1. Take turns choosing four words from road signs.
2. Give those words to another player who will have one minute to turn the words into a four-line rhyming poem using one word per line.

Eating the Alphabet Game

To start, the first player says, "I'm so hungry I could eat an apple" (or anteater, or alligator). The second player then has to choose something beginning with the next letter of the alphabet, adding to the first player's choice: "I'm so hungry I could eat an apple and a balloon," and so on. See if your family can make it to Z, with each player remembering all the items that came before: "apple, balloon…zebra!"

What is your favourite food?

_____

_____

_____

_____

Can you think of some of your
own fun games to play?

_____

_____

_____

_____

_____

_____

_____

_____

WRITE!

Today's date: _____

What Canada means to me

_____
_____
_____
_____
_____
_____
_____
_____
_____
_____
_____
_____
_____
_____
_____

DRAW!

Today's date: _____

Today we went to

My favourite thing about today was

My least favourite thing about today was

_____

_____

_____

_____

_____

_____

_____

_____

Would I visit here again? Why or why not?

_____

_____

_____

_____

_____

_____

_____

WRITE!

Today's date: _____

_____

_____

_____

_____

_____

_____

_____

_____

_____

_____

_____

_____

_____

_____

_____

DRAW!

Today's date: _____

Let's go CAMPING in the Canadian outdoors

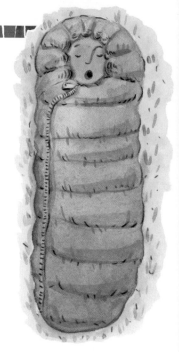

Mountains, prairies, lakes, rivers, and forests characterize Canada's natural and breathtaking landscape.

Canada is home to a number of national parks, such as Yoho, Point Pelee, Jasper, Quttinirpaaq, and Gros Morne. These National Parks conserve and protect forests, lakes, and wildlife. You may be interested in exploring the Rocky Mountains, the Atlantic or Pacific shore, or even the Arctic.

Have you ever gone camping? These national parks are wonderful places for you and your family to go for a camping trip! But until then, you can go camping in your own backyard...

Write about your camping experiences, or where you hope to go camping someday.

Outside and Inside S'mores

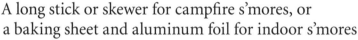

You'll need

Marshmallows
Graham crackers, broken in halves
Chocolate bars, broken in halves
A long stick or skewer for campfire s'mores, or
a baking sheet and aluminum foil for indoor s'mores

HOW TO MAKE CAMPFIRE S'MORES

Get your graham crackers and chocolate ready first.
Lay a chocolate bar half on one graham cracker half and have another
graham cracker half ready to go. Now put a marshmallow on the end of
your stick and hold over the fire, turning to keep it browning nicely and
evenly on all sides. It's finished when it's brown all over and a little crispy
on the outside. Now have a friend sandwich the marshmallow between
the graham and chocolate halves while you pull your stick out of the
marshmallow. Now you have a s'more!

HOW TO MAKE S'MORES IN THE OVEN

Heat oven to 350 degrees Fahrenheit (180 degrees Celsius). Line a
baking sheet with foil. Lay cracker halves on baking sheet, top with
chocolate bar halves, then marshmallows. Toast in oven for about 5
minutes, just until marshmallow is melty and chocolate begins to
soften. Remove from oven and top with another graham cracker half.
S'mores indoors all year round!

WRITE!

Today's date: _____

_____

_____

_____

_____

_____

_____

_____

_____

_____

_____

_____

_____

_____

_____

_____

_____

DRAW!

Today's date: _____

When I grow up I want to be

A place I want to go someday

WRITE!

Today's date: _____

DRAW!

Today's date: _____

If I wrote a book it would be about

_____

_____

_____

_____

_____

_____

_____

_____

_____

_____

If I made a movie, it would be about

_____

_____

_____

If I made a TV show, it would be about

_____

_____

_____

If I could star in a movie, I would star as a

_____

_____

_____

If I could star in a TV show, I would star as a

_____

_____

_____

I think it would be fun to be an actor because

_____

_____

_____

WRITE!

Today's date: _____

_____

_____

_____

_____

_____

_____

_____

_____

_____

_____

_____

_____

_____

_____

DRAW!

Today's date: _____

Today we went to

_____

_____

_____

_____

My favourite thing about today was

_____

_____

_____

_____

_____

_____

_____

100 _____

_____

My least favourite thing about today was

Would I visit here again? Why or why not?

WRITE!

Today's date: _____

What I love about Canada

_____

_____

_____

_____

_____

_____

_____

_____

_____

_____

_____

_____

_____

_____

What I love about my province

_____

_____

_____

_____

_____

_____

_____

What I love about my city

_____

_____

_____

_____

_____

_____

_____

_____

DRAW!

Today's date: _____

What do you love about going
back to school?

School days

My favourite subject in school

_____

_____

_____

My least favourite subject in school

_____

_____

_____

If I were a teacher, I would

_____

_____

_____

If I could change one thing about school, I would

_____

_____

_____

The thing I like most about school

_____

_____

_____

WRITE!

Today's date: _____

_____

_____

_____

_____

_____

_____

_____

_____

_____

_____

_____

_____

_____

_____

DRAW!

Today's date: _____

WRITE!

Today's date: _____

A place I hope to go someday

_____

_____

_____

If I could live anywhere in the world I'd choose

_____

_____

_____

Someone I wish lived near me

_____

_____

_____

Of all the places I've been, I liked this best

_____

_____

_____

Of all the places I've been, I really didn't like

_____

_____

If I could change one thing
about where I live it would be

_____

_____

_____

_____

_____

_____

_____

_____

_____

115

WRITE!

Today's date: _____

_____

_____

_____

_____

_____

_____

_____

_____

_____

_____

_____

_____

_____

_____

_____

DRAW!

Today's date: _____

Can you write your own poem? Here's how.

1st Stanza

I am.. (*two special characteristics you have*)

I wonder .... (*something you are actually curious about*)

I hear .... (*an imaginary sound*)

I see .... (*an imaginary sight*)

I want.. (*an actual desire*)

I am... (*the first line of the poem repeated*)

2nd Stanza

I pretend................................. (*something you actually pretend to do*)

I feel .... (*a feeling about something imaginary*)

I touch... (*an imaginary touch*)

I worry .... (*something that really bothers you*)

I cry............................... (*something that makes you very sad*)

I am........................... (*the first line of the poem repeated*)

3rd Stanza

I understand .... (*something you know is true*)

I say.. (*something you believe in*)

I dream................................. (*something you actually dream about*)

I try .... (*something you really make an effort about*)

I hope.. (*something you actually hope for*)

I am... (*the first line of the poem repeated*)

Now, write your own poem here:

1st Stanza

I am _____

I wonder _____

I hear _____

I see _____

I want _____

I am _____

2nd Stanza

I pretend _____

I feel _____

I touch _____

I worry _____

I cry _____

I am _____

3rd Stanza

I understand _____

I say _____

I dream _____

I try _____

I hope _____

I am _____

WRITE!

Today's date: _____

DRAW!

Today's date: _____

Do you know the name of Canada's capital city? **Ottawa!** — in the winter it is home to the world's largest skating rink!

In the wintertime you can bring your skates to Ottawa and skate on the Rideau Canal for 7.8 kilometres. Be sure to stop for a special treat—a delicious fried pastry in the shape of a beaver tail with sugar, cinnamon, or jam toppings—mmmmm!!

Ottawa is located in the province of Ontario and was chosen as the capital city by Queen Victoria in 1857. Ottawa is home to Parliament Hill—where the offices of our government officials are located. Our Prime Minister lives in Ottawa with his family at 24 Sussex Drive.

Tulips!

Each year in May Ottawa hosts one of the world's largest festivals—the annual Canadian Tulip Festival. During this festival over 1 million colourful tulips are in bloom. The tulip is Ottawa's official flower. Write and illustrate an original poem about tulips.

What makes YOU a Canadian kid?